FIRST PEOPLES

THE KURDS

OF ASIA

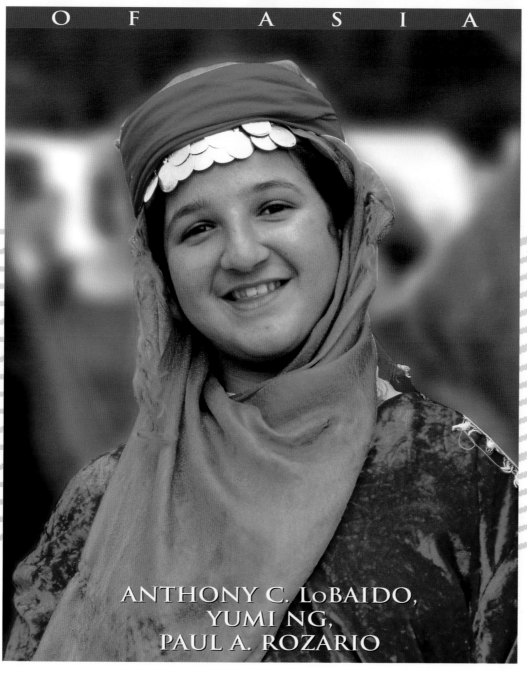

ANTHONY C. LoBAIDO,
YUMI NG,
PAUL A. ROZARIO

Lerner Publications Company • Minneapolis

**First American edition published in 2003
by Lerner Publications Company**

Published by arrangement with Times Editions
Copyright © 2003 by Times Media Private Limited

Lerner Publications Company
A division of Lerner Publishing Group
241 First Avenue North
Minneapolis, MN 55401 U.S.A.
Website address: www.lernerbooks.com

Series originated and designed by
Times Editions
An imprint of Times Media Private Limited
A member of the Times Publishing Group
1 New Industrial Road, Singapore 536196
Website address: www.timesone.com.sg/te

Series editors: Margaret J. Goldstein, Paul A. Rozario
Series designers: Tuck Loong, Geoslyn Lim
Series picture researcher: Susan Jane Manuel

Library of Congress Cataloging-in-Publication Data
LoBaido, Anthony C.
The Kurds of Asia / by Anthony C. LoBaido, Yumi Ng, and Paul A. Rozario.
p. cm. — (First peoples)
Includes bibliographical references and index.
Summary: Describes the history, modern and traditional
cultural practices and economies, geographic background,
and ongoing oppression and struggles of the Kurds.
ISBN 0-8225-0664-5 (lib. bdg. : alk. paper)
1. Kurds—Asia. 2. Kurds—Middle East. [1. Kurds.] I. Ng, Yumi.
II. Rozario, Paul. III. Title. IV. Series.
DS59.K86 L63 2003
950'.0491597—dc21   2002006471

Printed in Malaysia
Bound in the United States of America

1 2 3 4 5 6—0S—08 07 06 05 04 03

CONTENTS

WHO ARE THE KURDS?

The Kurds are an ancient people from western Asia. The Kurds do not have a country of their own. They live in a vast area that covers parts of western Turkey, northern Iraq, and northwestern Iran. This area, called Kurdistan, covers about 200,000 square miles (518,000 square kilometers). There are also small Kurdish communities in northeastern Syria, Armenia, and Azerbaijan, as well as other former Soviet republics. Other small communities of Kurds are found in Western Europe and North America.

A Nation with No Boundaries

Kurdistan means "land of the Kurds" in Arabic. The region has no exact boundaries. It stretches roughly from southeastern Turkey, near the eastern end of the Mediterranean Sea, to the Pontic Mountains in northern Turkey and the Zagros Mountains in Iran. In ancient times, Kurdistan was a commercial center. It was located along the Silk Road, a trading route between Asia and Europe. Traders passing through Kurdistan purchased rugs and handicrafts from the Kurds.

THE KURDS AND THEIR NEIGHBORS

Kurdistan is home to about 35 million Kurds; more than half of them live in Turkey. The Kurds share their lands with three other large ethnic groups: the Arabs, who mainly inhabit Iraq and other Middle Eastern nations; the Turks, who mainly inhabit Turkey; and the Persians, who mainly inhabit Iran. Kurdish people make up about 20 percent of the population of Turkey, 23 percent of Iraq, and 7 percent of Iran. For many years, the Kurds have been oppressed in their host countries. Present-day Kurds continue to fight to obtain cultural and political rights in Turkey, Iraq, Syria, and Iran.

LAND OF MOUNTAINS AND VALLEYS

Kurdistan is very mountainous. It is located in an active seismic zone, which means that earthquakes occur there often. High in the mountains, the weather is very cold. Snow covers the upper slopes for up to seven months a year. The average winter temperature in the mountains is about 40 degrees Fahrenheit (4 degrees Celsius). The weather is warmer on lower slopes and at the foot of the mountains. Summers in Kurdistan are hot and dry.

Below: Snow melts on mountaintops in Kurdistan.

Towering Peaks

Above: Mount Damavand, the highest peak in Iran, rises majestically in Iranian Kurdistan.

The Southeastern Taurus Mountains and the Pontic Mountains in Turkey, the Zagros Mountains in northern Iraq, and the Elburz Mountains in northern Iran are the main mountain ranges in Kurdistan. The tallest mountain in Turkish Kurdistan is Mount Ararat, at 16,941 feet (5,163 meters). The tallest mountain in Iraqi Kurdistan is Mount Ebrahim, at 11,644 feet (3,549 meters). At 18,934 feet (5,771 meters), Mount Damavand in the Elburz Mountains is the highest peak in Iran. The Kurds have been living in this area for centuries. So they are used to living, working, and fighting in the mountains.

Forests, Fields, and Foothills

Large areas of Kurdistan are covered with trees. Poplar and oak forests grow in the valleys of northern Iraq. The Tigris, Great Zab, Little Zab, and Diyala Rivers flow down from the Zagros Mountains, making the soil rich and fertile. The Kurds grow tobacco, grain, vines, and fruit in the rich soil. They also take cattle and sheep to graze on the foothills and fields.

Right: Kurdistan has many lush forests.

LIFE IN AN EARTHQUAKE ZONE

Many earthquakes occur in northeastern Kurdistan, along the North Anatolian Fault, a crack in the earth's surface. This area has suffered many earthquakes throughout history, and the quakes have destroyed numerous ancient monuments there. A devastating earthquake took place there in 1939, killing more than 30,000 people.

PRECIOUS RESOURCES

Kurdistan is rich in many resources, including water, oil, natural gas, and valuable metals and minerals. Many of these resources have yet to be tapped. These resources would be a good source of income for Kurdistan if the Kurds were able to gain independence.

Below: The Euphrates River flows through Kurdistan.

Above: Pipelines in Iraqi Kurdistan transport oil and natural gas to other parts of Iraq.

Valuable Water

The Tigris and Euphrates Rivers begin in Kurdistan, high in the mountains of eastern Turkey. These rivers flow down from the mountains and water the plains of Iraq before flowing into the Persian Gulf. The oldest civilizations in the Middle East began in the fertile plains around the Tigris and Euphrates Rivers. This area is known as the Fertile Crescent. Lake Urmia, Iran's largest lake, is located near Kurdistan. The rivers and lakes of Kurdistan are important natural resources. People use these bodies of water for fishing, transportation, drinking, and farming. Rivers also provide hydroelectricity— electric power created by rushing water.

Oil and Minerals

The soil of Iranian Kurdistan is rich in oil. The Iranian government and international oil companies extract most of the oil and keep the profits themselves. The Kurds seldom benefit from this resource. Iranian Kurdistan is also rich in natural gas. Iraqi Kurdistan has rich oilfields in the valleys and foothills of the Zagros Mountains. It is also rich in iron and chrome, but these minerals have not yet been mined.

CONTROL OF KURDISTAN'S RICHES

The governments of Turkey, Iran, and Iraq want to control the rich natural resources found in Kurdistan, such as oil, minerals, and water (*right*). The governments want to keep these valuable resources for themselves. They do not want Kurdistan to become an independent country and claim these resources for the Kurds.

MOUNTAIN FLORA AND FAUNA

Starting in spring, all sorts of wildflowers and plants bloom in Kurdistan. Trees such as oaks, poplars, and chestnuts grow in the forests. Ash, juniper, cedar, and pine trees grow in the mountains.

Animals on the Land

Kurdistan has a great variety of animal life. The Kurds raise cattle, goats, and sheep in the mountains and on the plains. Bears, beavers, foxes, cheetahs, boars, wolves, leopards, deer, jackals, and lynxes also roam Kurdistan. Antelopes, ibexes, wild ass, wild pigs, and wild goats live in Iranian Kurdistan. As more forests are cleared, however, animals have fewer places to live. Animal populations are shrinking in Kurdistan, especially numbers of large cats such cheetahs, leopards, and lynxes.

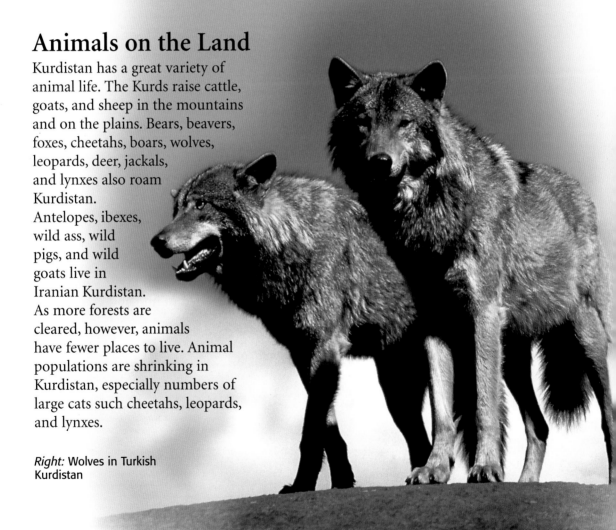

Right: Wolves in Turkish Kurdistan

Above: Flamingos wade through a marsh in Iranian Kurdistan.

Animals in the Air

Many different bird species live in Kurdistan, including eagles, storks, vultures, larks, bluebirds, and the bald ibis. Ducks and geese live in swamps and near rivers. Kurdistan is also home to many migratory birds—birds that spend only part of the year in Kurdistan.

Animals in the Water

The rivers of Kurdistan teem with many varieties of fish. The Kurds catch these fish for food. Whitefish, herring, and salmon make their homes in mountain streams and rivers. Otters live in the rivers of the Zagros Mountains. Sturgeon live in the waters of the Caspian Sea, off the northern coast of Iran.

ENVIRONMENTAL DESTRUCTION

Abundant forests once covered the mountains of Kurdistan. But, over the years, the Kurds have cut down many trees and used the wood as fuel. Many mountains have become barren (*below*). Overgrazing on hills—allowing animals to eat too much grass—is another cause of deforestation. The animals that inhabit Kurdistan's forests have been hurt as well, since they cannot survive on barren land. In some places, especially in Iranian Kurdistan, people have created wildlife sanctuaries to protect land, animals, and plants.

THE ANCIENT KURDS

Kurdistan and the surrounding areas have been conquered and ruled by many different empires in the course of their history. These empires include the Babylonian, Assyrian, Greek, Roman, and Persian Empires in ancient times and the Ottoman Empire in more recent times.

Right: Cuneiform writing on a Sumerian tablet. Kurdistan lies in the Fertile Crescent, which was the birthplace of writing.

Below: A detail from a Persian carving. The Persians were one of many empires that ruled Kurdistan in ancient times.

Early Written Records

The Kurds have lived in western Asia for thousands of years. However, little is known for certain about their ancestors. The ancient Kurds left very few written records. Most records were kept by other civilizations and mention the Kurds only in passing. The earliest mention of the Kurds is found in Sumerian writings dating to 3000 B.C. In these records, the Sumerians refer to Kurdistan as the "land of Karda." In his book *Anabasis*, the Greek historian Xenophon wrote about a group of Kurds who attacked the retreating armies of Persian king Cyrus in 400 B.C.

On the Fringes of Empires

The Kurds have always lived in rugged mountain locations. It has been difficult for ruling armies to reach Kurdish towns. As a result, ruling empires did not exercise complete control over Kurdish territory. Instead, rulers allowed the Kurds considerable freedom. For most of their history, the Kurds enjoyed an independent lifestyle. Their own leaders controlled the day-to-day activities of their communities, such as water distribution and farming. For the most part, ruling empires were content to leave the Kurds in peace, as long as the Kurds paid taxes and traded with them.

Above: This mosaic shows Alexander the Great, who rode through Kurdistan in around 333 B.C.

THE FIRST CIVILIZATION

The world's earliest civilization started around 3500 B.C. in the fertile region around the Tigris and Euphrates Rivers. Part of this area is present-day Kurdistan. Scholars believe that ancestors of the Kurds belonged to this first civilization. They were among first people in the world to farm, engage in trade, and live in cities.

THE KURDS AMID POWERFUL EMPIRES

In the first century B.C.., the Romans conquered present-day Turkey. By the A.D. 400s, the West Roman Empire had died out. But the East Roman Empire continued, with Turkey as its center. The East Roman Empire is more commonly known as the Byzantine Empire.

The Coming of Islam

In the A.D. 600s, Arab armies conquered large parts of the Middle East, including Kurdistan. The Arabs converted the majority of the Kurds to Islam, a religion founded by the prophet Muhammad. Kurdistan became a border between the Christian Byzantine Empire on the west and the Islamic Empire on the east. Kurdish warriors were famous for their toughness and military skill. The different empires often employed Kurds to guard their borders.

Below: The mosque of Dogubeyazit in Turkish Kurdistan was built by a Kurdish chieftain in the 1700s.

New Rulers

In the 1300s, the Ottomans, a group of Islamic Turks, came to power in northwestern Turkey. They quickly expanded their territory. They defeated the Byzantine Empire in 1453. At its peak, the Ottoman Empire extended over much of Eastern Europe, parts of the Middle East, and North Africa. From the 1400s until the 1800s, about three-quarters of Kurdistan was under Ottoman control, while one-quarter was under Persian control.

Left: A sixteenth-century painting shows Ottoman soldiers capturing a castle in Turkey.

Right: The ruins of an Ottoman castle in Turkish Kurdistan

An Independent People

Even under Persian and Ottoman control, the Kurds continued to enjoy self-rule. In many cases, Kurdish leaders agreed to work for the governments of ruling empires. This arrangement suited all parties: The Kurdish leaders could retain power in their villages. The empires were spared the cost and trouble of sending troops to mountainous Kurdish territory to ensure obedience. The common people were glad to be ruled by their own leaders.

A GREAT KURD COMMANDER

From 1095 to 1270, Christian armies from Europe tried to take back Jerusalem and other areas of the Middle East from Islamic rulers. This campaign was known as the Crusades. In 1169 a Kurdish commander named Saladin helped defend Egypt from the European armies. He then embarked on a campaign that united the Islamic territories of Syria, northern Mesopotamia, Kurdistan, Palestine, and Egypt. Saladin is remembered for his wisdom, compassion, and good leadership.

A NATION DIVIDED

In the 1800s, the Ottoman Empire began to decline. The empire suffered from problems such as overpopulation, unemployment, and religious riots. The final blow to the Ottoman Empire came in World War I (1914–1918), when it was defeated along with Germany and the other Central Powers.

Below: This sculpture in the Turkish city of Istanbul shows the founding leaders of the Turkish state.

Dividing the Empire

In 1918, after the Ottoman Empire's defeat, the victorious powers, including Great Britain and France, broke western Asia and the Middle East and into many different countries, including Turkey, Iraq, Syria, and Iran. One document, the Treaty of Sèvres, called for the creation of an independent state in Kurdistan, but the treaty was not enforced. Instead, Kurdistan was divided between Turkey, Iraq, Syria, and Iran.

Above: Iranian Kurds pose with the flag of the Mahabad Republic in 1946 .

The Mahabad Republic

From December 1945 to December 1946, the Kurds' dream of having their own state was realized on a small scale in Iran. During World War II, British and Soviet forces attacked Iran. The Soviets took control of parts of northern Iran, while the British took control of the southern area. With Iran defeated, no real power controlled the area between the Soviet- and British-occupied regions. The Kurds took advantage of this vacuum to form the Mahabad Republic, an independent Kurdish state with its capital at the city of Mahabad. After about a year, however, Iran took back control of the area.

Right: The flag of the Mahabad Republic

A KURD HERO

An Iraqi Kurd named Mustafa Barzani served as army commander of the short-lived Mahabad Republic. After Iran defeated the republic, Barzani took refuge in the Soviet Union. In 1958, he went back to Iraq, where he began a guerrilla war against the Iraqi government, again trying to create an autonomous Kurdish state. The conflict lasted from 1960 to 1975, when Iraqi troops finally defeated Barzani's forces. He eventually sought safe haven in the United States, where he died in 1979.

STRUGGLING TO SURVIVE

Since the end of World War I, the Kurds have tried to establish their own state. But the governments of Turkey, Iran, and Iraq have denied them an independent homeland. These governments have often treated the Kurds harshly. They have used violence to maintain control over Kurdish communities.

The Kurds in Turkey

Turkey is home to more than 15 million Kurds, or about one-fifth of the total Turkish population. Starting in the 1920s, the Turkish government set out to modernize Turkey. The government wanted the Kurds to assimilate—or mix in with other Turks—and forget their Kurdish heritage. The government forbade Kurds to use their own language. Kurds were forced from their homes in the countryside into towns and cities. In 1984 the Kurdistan Workers' Party (PKK), established in 1978, started a series of terror attacks on Turkish officials and civilians. The government responded violently. To this date, thousands of people have been killed in the struggle between the Kurds and the Turkish state.

Below: British Kurds protest in the streets of central London, England.

The Kurds in Iraq

Up until the late 1950s, the Kurds in Iraq enjoyed a certain amount of freedom. In 1958, rebels killed Iraq's king and took over the government. The new Iraqi government was more hostile to the Kurds. It destroyed Kurdish villages and sent the Kurds to live in Arab areas. During the 1960s and 1970s, the Kurds revolted several times without success. In 1980 war broke out between Iraq and Iran. Iraq's Kurds sided with Iran in the fighting. After the war, the Iraqi government punished the Kurds, killing thousands with poison gas. To escape government troops, many Kurds fled to Iran and Turkey. Iraqi Kurds rebelled again after the Persian Gulf War in 1991, but Iraqi troops quickly put down the rebellion. Again, many Kurds fled Iraq. Aided by the nations that fought Iraq in 1991, most Iraqi Kurds have since returned to their homes.

Below: Kurdish soldiers resting on a hillside in northern Iraq

The Kurds in Iran

Following the defeat of the Mahabad Republic in 1946, the government of Iran continued to deny the Kurdish people independence. Under Mohammad Reza's rule (1941–1979), some Kurds were allowed to hold high government and military jobs. Revolutionaries overthrew Iran's government in 1979, and the new government was less tolerant of the Kurds. Kurds in present-day Iran number more than four million. They enjoy some limited freedom, but the government still opposes any move toward Kurdish independence.

POLITICAL PRISONER

Leyla Zana, a Kurdish member of the Turkish parliament, has been a leader in the struggle for Kurdish independence. In 1994 she was sentenced to fifteen years in prison for speaking in Kurdish in parliament. In 1995 the European Parliament gave Zana an award called the Sakharov Prize for her efforts to gain more rights for the Kurds in a peaceful, political manner.

FROM TRADITIONAL TO NEW OCCUPATIONS

T he Kurdish economy remained more or less unchanged for centuries. Traditionally, Kurds worked as farmers, herders, and traders. Some Kurds were nomads—they traveled from place to place, searching for fresh pastures for their animals. In the twentieth century, life changed for the Kurds. Because of war and government oppression, many Kurds were forced to leave their homes and farms in the countryside. Many moved to cities and took up new occupations. Other Kurds were able to stay in their traditional villages. They continue to work as their ancestors did.

Left: A Kurdish vendor in Iraqi Kurdistan

Rural Life in Kurdistan

Most Kurds who live in the countryside work as farmers. Kurdistan has a variety of different climates, good rainfall, and fertile soil. Crops grown in Kurdistan include wheat, rice, millet, squash, tomatoes, and tobacco. Kurdish farmers also grow many kinds of fruit, such as apricots, apples, pears, and figs. Other Kurds in the countryside work as shepherds. They herd flocks of sheep, goats, and cattle across mountains and valleys. These animals provide the Kurds with milk, yogurt, meat, and skins.

Trading and Commerce

In the past, Kurdistan lay at the center of trade routes between Asia, Europe, and the Middle East. These routes are still used in modern times, and many Kurds still work as traders. They travel from place to place, selling and exchanging goods from Kurdistan and other regions. Some Kurdish traders set up shops in Kurdish towns and cities and sell their goods there.

Left: A Kurdish herdsman drives his flock of goats across a dry plain in Iranian Kurdistan.

Above: A Kurdish nomad weaves a basket outside his tent in eastern Turkey.

MIGRATION TO THE CITIES

In Iraq and Turkey, the government has destroyed many Kurdish villages over the years. Officials have resettled Kurds into towns and cities, where residents can be better controlled and are less likely to rebel. Kurds who live in cities work in many fields, including teaching, law, business, medicine, and politics.

ECONOMIC STRUGGLES

Kurdistan's economy, like its territory, is divided up between three main countries—Iran, Iraq, and Turkey. Officials from these countries make economic decisions for Kurdistan. But these decisions don't always benefit the Kurds.

Poverty Amid Riches

The oilfields of Kurdistan produce more than half of Iraq's oil. In fact, one of the world's richest oilfields lies near the Kurdish city of Kirkuk, Iraq. However, the Kurds do not receive income from the sale of this valuable oil. That money goes to the Iraqi government and big oil companies. The Kurdish people of Iraq remain very poor.

Right: Kurdish nomads in southern Iran draw water from a well.

Who Controls Water?

The Tigris, Euphrates, and other rivers of Kurdistan are valuable resources. The rivers provide water for drinking and hydroelectric power. The Turkish, Iraqi, and Iranian governments sell this power and water to nearby countries, such as Saudi Arabia, Israel, and Jordan. The Kurds do not benefit from the sale of these resources.

Right: The Karadj Dam in the Elburz Mountains in Iranian Kuridistan

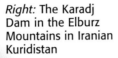

OIL-FOR-FOOD PROGRAM

Iraq's people suffered greatly during and after the Persian Gulf War. Crises included food shortages and outbreaks of disease. In 1996, the United Nations began the Oil-for-Food program to assist the Iraqi people. Under this program, many Iraqis receive health care, food, and other assistance from the UN. The money for the program comes from the sale of Iraq's valuable oil. This program has been beneficial to the Iraqi Kurds (*below*). Infant mortality, or death, rates have fallen since the program began. Iraqi Kurdistan's economy has improved.

MANY TRIBES AND CLANS

Kurdish society is composed of more than 800 tribes. Tribes are further divided into clans, or large family groups. Some tribes consist of only one clan. Other tribes are made up of several clans. Kurds are usually extremely loyal to their fellow clan and tribe members.

Above: A village leader in Iraqi Kurdistan

Leaving Their Homelands

In the past, different clans lived in different parts of Kurdistan. They were usually separated by geographical features such as mountains, rivers, and valleys. In the 1900s, the government forced many Kurds to leave their traditional homelands. Many clans were split apart.

Above: Kurdish soldiers pose in northern Iraq.

Kurdish Chieftains

Left: Women in Iraqi Kurdistan collect drinking water.

Most Kurdish clans are ruled by a chief, called an emir. In the past, clan chiefs formed alliances with other chiefs. The allied clans supported local leaders, who in turn supported the major kingdoms of the time. Even in modern times, clan chiefs still play an important leadership role in Kurdish life.

NEW ALLIANCES

In modern times, Kurdish clans often unite through political parties. Iraq's Kurdish Democratic Party, for instance, is supported mainly by the Barzani clan and is led by Masoud Barzani (*right*). Other Kurdish political parties include the Kurdistan Workers' Party in Turkey and the Patriotic Union of Kurdistan in Iraq.

FAMILY LIFE

Above: A Kurdish bride and her attendants

I n a Kurdish family, a person's age and gender determine his or her responsibilities. In a traditional family, the father is the undisputed head of the household. He earns an income and provides for his wife and children. The mother takes care of the children and the home.

Mothers and Daughters

A Kurdish daughter lives in her father's house until marriage. When she marries, she does not change her name. In this way, she honors her parents and family. After giving birth, a woman will spend forty days in her original family's home. Her sisters and mother will look after all her needs during this time.

Below: Kurdish boys in Izmir, Turkey, play a game of marbles.

Brothers and Sisters

Parents pass on Kurdish traditions to their children. Sons honor their fathers and may take up their fathers' occupations. Daughters help their mothers in caring for the family and home. They are encouraged to be loving and compassionate. Brothers look out for their sisters and honor and protect them. Both boys and girls go to school.

Left: A Kurdish woman prepares bread for her family.

Below: A Kurdish family in Iraqi Kurdistan

Marriage Traditions

Traditional Kurdish marriages are colorful affairs that last many days. They feature feasting, singing, and dancing. Kurds tend to marry within their own clans. Marriages are usually arranged by the parents of the bride and groom. However, as more Kurds move from their traditional homelands to cities, and as Kurdish society becomes more modern, some marriage traditions are changing.

CHANGING VALUES

Some Kurdish people have moved to the United States, Australia, and Europe. There, they live in communities that are not as traditional as Kurdish society. Because of modern influences, young Kurds growing up outside Kurdistan sometimes abandon some of their parents' traditions.

EXTRAORDINARY WOMEN

Throughout history, Kurdish women have played important roles in areas usually dominated by men. These areas include the military, politics, business, and religion. Stories of the brave deeds of Kurdish women go back to ancient times.

Below: Kurdish women clap and sing around a Kurdish bride.

Women in Politics

Kurdish women have also been active in the political arena. Women ruled many medieval Kurdish kingdoms. In the 1800s, a woman named Kara Fatima represented the Kurds at the Ottoman court in Constantinople. More recently, Kurdish politician Leyla Zana has become famous for her peaceful efforts on behalf of Kurds in Turkey.

Above: A Kurdish woman joins a procession in the Turkish city of Diyarbakir.

Women Warriors

In Greek mythology, the Amazons were a tribe of fierce women warriors. Perhaps this legend originated with tales of Kurd female fighters. According to the Greek historian Plutarch, women in western Kurdistan fought fiercely against invading Roman troops in 100 B.C. Plutarch also said that Roman soldiers were impressed by the fighting skills of the wife of a Kurdish ruler. Modern Kurdish women continue to play important roles in the military. Many Kurdish guerrilla groups include female soldiers. Turkey's PKK has had large numbers of women in its armed units.

Right: An elderly Kurd woman. Older Kurds are respected for their wisdom and experience.

SUCCESS IN BUSINESS

In ancient times, many Kurdish women were wealthy and prominent business-women. Under the Islamic religion, practiced by most modern-day Kurds, women's lives are more restricted. Yet some wealthy Kurdish women still run businesses, sometimes in a secretive way.

CUSTOMS AND COURTESIES

The Kurds are a very polite people. When conducting business, Kurds always treat their business partners with respect. They value humility, morals, manners, and good ethics. To lie or cheat in a business deal brings great shame to one's self and perhaps the family name.

Below: A Kurdish family receives blessings as they enter a Yezidi temple in Iraqi Kurdistan.

Visiting Friends

Kurds enjoy visiting friends and neighbors, especially someone who is ill or has just returned from a journey. Kurds often bring foods, flowers, sweets, and drinks to friends who are sick. Kurdish hosts offer coffee, tea, and sweets to visitors.

Right: Kurdish men sit down to a meal in Turkish Kurdistan.

A Generous People

The Kurds are very generous. If you visit a Kurd's home and openly state that you like a furnishing or another possession, the homeowner might well want to give you that item. So outsiders who visit with Kurds should be careful not to focus too much attention on their hosts' possessions.

TIPS FOR VISITORS

Outsiders who visit a Kurdish family (*left*) must never hug or kiss any female member, even with just a friendly peck on the cheek. Such contact is considered improper and may insult the head of the household. Likewise, foreigners who do business with Kurdish women should avoid hugging or kissing them. It is acceptable to shake the hand of a Kurdish woman, however, if she offers it in a greeting.

KURDISH HOMES

Above: The simple interior of a house inhabited by an elderly Kurdish couple in eastern Turkey

The shape and style of traditional Kurdish homes varied according to location. Nomadic Kurds—Kurds who roamed the mountains in search of fresh pastures for their herds—traditionally lived in tents. But most Kurds lived in homes made from mud, bricks, or both. These homes had straw roofs and were very sturdy. Many present-day Kurds still live in mud-brick homes. Some Kurdish homes have modern comforts such as electricity, running water, and satellite television.

Beehive Dwellings

Some Kurds, mostly in Turkey, live in beehive, or dome-shaped, homes. The walls of these homes are made of dried animal dung mixed with straw and other materials. Beehive homes are not very large. They usually house a single family.

Below: Eastern Turkey is home to Kurdish nomads who live in tents.

Homes on Hillsides

The Kurds in Iran and Iraq live in flat houses built in levels. These homes are built on hillsides, so that the roof of one level of homes forms the ground floor for another level of homes. People enter their homes either by walking through the front entrance or climbing down a ladder through the roof.

Above: These hillside homes are found in Iranian Kurdistan.

Simple Is Good

Kurdish homes are simple. Some families eat at tables and chairs, but most Kurds eat while sitting on rugs on the floor. Instead of beds, most Kurds sleep on mats, which they can easily roll up and put away during the daytime. Homes are decorated with colorful wall hangings.

Left: The wall above the door of this Kurdish house is decorated with colorful symbols.

NEW KURDISH TOWNS

In recent years, the Turkish government has forced many Kurds to leave their homes in the countryside. The Kurds have been forced to move into towns, where they live in simple concrete dwellings. The Kurds are not free to leave town without permission. The Turkish army enforces strict curfews for Kurds who need to attend to business or personal matters outside of town.

THE LANGUAGE OF THE KURDS

The Kurdish language belongs to the Indo-European family of languages. Kurdish is related to Farsi, the national language of Iran. Kurdish is divided into two main dialects, or variations. These dialects are Kurmanji and Sorani. Although Kurmanji and Sorani share many similar words, they do not have the same grammar. Therefore, Kurmanji-speaking Kurds and Sorani-speaking Kurds often cannot understand one another. In addition, Kurmanji is written in Roman letters, the same alphabet used in English. Sorani is written in Arabic letters—a completely different alphabet.

Below: Kurdish children in Izmir, Turkey, do not study Kurdish in schools. Instead, they learn the language from their parents and grandparents.

Kurmanji

Above: A Kurdish man reads the Quran, the sacred text of Islam.

Kurmanji, also called Northern Kurdish, is spoken by Kurds in Turkey, northern Iraq, Syria, Armenia, and the Iranian province of Khorasan. Small numbers of Kurmanji speakers also live in the former Soviet republics of Georgia and Azerbaijan, as well as in Lebanon, Europe, and North America. In the 1920s, the Turkish government restricted the use of Kurmanji. Kurds were supposed to speak only Turkish. Most Kurds who live in big Turkish cities speak both Kurmanji and Turkish. Many young Kurdish people are more fluent in Turkish than Kurmanji.

Sorani

Sorani is also called Southern Kurdish. Kurds in Iraq and Iran are the main Sorani speakers. Unlike Turkey, Iran and Iraq have never restricted the use of Sorani. Kurdish children in Iran and Iraq learn Sorani in school. Newspapers and books are written in Sorani. Radio and television stations broadcast in Sorani as well.

Learn to Speak Kurdish

English	Kurmanji	Pronunciation	Sorani	Pronunciation
bread	*nan*	NAHN	*nan*	NAHN
brother	*bira*	BEH-rah	*bra*	BRAH
child	*zar*	ZAHR	*mindal*	MIN-dahl
water	*av*	AHV	*aw*	OW
woman	*jin*	JEHN	*jin*	ZHIN

LITERATURE OF THE KURDS

The Kurds have a long literary tradition. Yasar Kemal (*right*), one of Turkey's most acclaimed novelists, is a Kurd. For the most part, Kurds have written in the major languages of their home territories: Turkish, Arabic, and Farsi. But some famous Kurdish writers have written in Kurmanji. They include Mulla Jaziri, a seventeenth-century poet, and Ahmad Khani, who wrote the *Mem-u Zin*, a long Kurdish poem.

KURDISH MUSIC AND DANCE

Music and dance are important parts of Kurdish life. Traditional Kurdish music varies according to region. The music and rhythms of mountain Kurds are different from those of Kurds who live in valleys and meadows. Kurds who have left Kurdistan still value music as a way to preserve Kurdish culture. Any social gathering of Kurdish people, even outside Kurdistan, usually features much dancing and singing.

Above: The Kamkars Group is one of the most famous Kurdish musical groups in the world.

Traditional Instruments

Kurdish musicians use a variety of instruments. The *daf* is a simple drum made of goat or lambskin stretched over a wooden frame. Metal pieces attached to the daf jingle when the instrument is played. The *tanbur* is a pear-shaped string instrument that is plucked or strummed. It usually has three strings. The top two play the melody, while bottom string provides a drone—an unchanging background note. In the hands of an expert player, the tanbur produces a very rich sound.

A Song for Every Occasion

The Kurds have a song for every occasion. These songs are called *gourani* and are based on Kurdish poems. Some gourani are sung during everyday activities, such as sheepherding and housework. Special gourani are sung during festivals, wedding, and funerals. Festive gourani have strong and exciting rhythms and are often accompanied by enthusiastic clapping and dancing. Romantic gourani speak of courting beautiful women and true love.

Above: Kurdish daf players lead a procession in Iraqi Kurdistan.

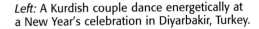
Left: A Kurdish couple dance energetically at a New Year's celebration in Diyarbakir, Turkey.

Joyous Dancing

Kurdish dances usually involve groups of people holding hands and dancing together in a circle. Occasionally, a couple will dance in the center of the circle. Some dances tell a story through the movement and actions of the dancers. One dance may depict courtship between a man and a woman. Another dance might show strong bonds between good friends.

SINGING BROTHERS

Metin and Kemal Kahraman are Kurdish musicians and brothers. They were born in southeastern Turkey, near the town of Dersim. They sing traditional Kurdish songs and play both modern and traditional Kurdish instruments. They sing in Kurdish as well as Turkish. Their music is inspired by the traditions, myths, and folktales of Dersim.

CARPETS AND COSTUMES

The Kurds have a long history of making arts and crafts. They are famous for creating beautiful carpets, rugs, and costumes. Rugs are made from the wool of sheep and are woven on traditional wooden looms. Kurdish costumes tend to be made from imported fabrics.

Colorful Kurdish Rugs

Kurds have been producing rugs for many hundreds of years. Rug makers are usually women, who make rugs for their immediate families or for sale in local markets. The patterns on rugs depict birds, stars, the Moon, flowers, and animals. Everyday objects such as combs and jewelry are also shown. The rugs are very colorful, with lots of bright red, blue, yellow, and pink shades, as well as geometric patterns.

Left: The colorful dress of a beautiful Kurdish woman and her baby

Beautiful Jewelry

In Kurdistan, both men and women wear jewelry. The jewelry of the Hakri tribe is among the most elaborate. A wealthy Hakri woman might wear many pounds of beads and brooches, made from precious metal and stones. Archaeologists have found jewelry at ancient Kurd burial grounds, showing that the Kurds have been wearing jewelry for many, many centuries.

Left: Kurdish women sometimes decorate their headdress with large coins.

Traditional Kurdish Dress

Traditional Kurdish costumes vary according to location. But certain styles have become widespread. For men, the most common clothes are a jacket worn with baggy trousers, which are gathered at the waist and ankles. Men also wear a sash around the waist and a turban of checkered cloth on the head. Kurdish women wear many different styles of dress, depending on where they live. Most women wear headdresses, large sashes around the waist, and long sleeves. The costumes are colorful, especially those worn during festivals and weddings.

Above: A Kurdish woman weaves a rug on a wooden loom.

KURDISH TATTOOS

Women in Syrian Kurdistan wear tattoos on their faces. The tattoos are made with an ink of milk and soot, applied with a needle. Older women (*left*) have elaborate star, diamond, and rectangle shapes tattooed below their mouths and on their chins. Young women have simpler tattoos on their chins. Hand and neck tattoos are also common.

NEW MEDIA, NEW MESSAGES

In earlier centuries, Kurdish stories and legends were passed down orally—by word of mouth. In modern times, people can learn about Kurdish culture through films, books, newspapers, and the Internet.

Kurdish Publishing

The first Kurdish book was printed in 1909 in Istanbul, Turkey. The first Kurdish publisher opened in Sulaymaniyah, Iraq, in 1920. Set up by the prominent Kurdish poet and writer Piramerd, this company produced books, newspapers, and journals about Kurdish culture. Other Kurdish publishers have since appeared in other parts of Kurdistan. Kurdish publishing has at times flourished and others times been suppressed, depending on government policies. Despite restrictions, many books are published in the Kurdish language.

Left: A satellite dish on a roof in Iraqi Kurdistan

Kurdish Film

Kurdish culture is also celebrated in film. But most Kurdish filmmakers live in North America and Europe, where there are fewer government restrictions on filmmaking. Many Kurdish films document the persecution that Kurds have endured throughout their long history.

Right: Director Kevin McKiernan receives an award for *Good Kurds, Bad Kurds*, a film that documents the struggle of the Kurdish people.

Television and Radio

Several television stations broadcast from Iraqi Kurdistan. Several Kurdish radio stations also operate in Kurdistan. But governments opposed to Kurdish independence frequency censor Kurdish TV and radio programs. The Turkish government often jams Kurdish radio and television signals. Between 1995 and 1999, Med TV, a United Kingdom–based Kurdish television channel, broadcast news and other programs in Europe.

INTO THE INTERNET AGE

With the dawn of the Internet, people have a new way to learn about Kurdish culture. Many websites document the difficult lives of the Kurds, as well as the harsh repression they have suffered at the hands of the Iraqi, Iranian, and Turkish governments. Other websites explain the traditional Kurdish way of life and the language and history of the Kurds. These websites help Kurds living outside of Kurdistan stay in touch with their language and cultural roots. Kurds within Kurdistan connect to the rest of the world at Internet cafés (*left*).

RELIGIOUS TRADITIONS

Above: A Kurdish mosque in Turkish Kurdistan

Right: A Kurd in Izmir, Turkey, prays using prayer beads.

Most present-day Kurds are Muslim, or followers of Islam. The majority of these Kurds follow the Sunni branch of Islam. There are also small numbers of Kurdish Christians, Jews, and Yezidis. Yezidis follow an ancient religion called the Cult of the Angels.

Followers of Islam

The Arabs brought Islam to Kurdistan in the seventh century A.D., and many Kurds embraced the new religion. Muslims worship one god, whom they call Allah. Muslims believe that Allah gave the prophet Muhammad a divine revelation. This revelation is found in the Quran, the Islamic holy book. Throughout history, the Kurds have contributed greatly to the expansion of Islam. Saladin was the most famous Kurdish Muslim. He founded the Kurdish Ayyubid dynasty, or ruling family, which reigned over the whole Muslim Middle East from 1169 to 1250.

Right: A Kurdish follower of the Yezidi religion

The Cult of the Angels

Before the coming of Islam, many Kurds were Yezidis—followers of the Cult of the Angels. The cult may have started in Kurdistan as early as 2000 B.C. Some Kurds still practice this faith. Yezidis believe in one god, and they believe this god created seven angels to help people in their everyday activities. Yezidi belief is closely related to Zoroastrianism, the ancient religion of Iran. The Yezidis form a small minority in Kurdistan. Because of religious persecution, many Yezidis have moved to Europe.

Kurds of Others Faiths

Small numbers of Kurds practice Judaism and Christianity. Most of these Kurds come from the mountainous and inaccessible region of northern Kurdistan. Because their communities are so remote, these Kurds have kept their Jewish and Christian beliefs and traditions, despite the dominance of Islam in the rest of Kurdistan.

THE FIVE PILLARS OF ISLAM

All Muslims must perform five acts of worship, called the Five Pillars of Islam. These acts are believing that there is no other god but Allah and that Muhammad was his prophet; praying in the direction of the holy city of Mecca, Saudi Arabia, five times a day; giving money to charity; fasting during Ramadan, the ninth month of the Islamic calendar; and going on a pilgrimage to Mecca at least once in a lifetime.

THE KURDISH NEW YEAR

The Kurds love to celebrate important events such as births and marriages. One of the most important Kurdish festivals is Nowruz, the Kurdish New Year. *Nowruz* means "new day" in the Kurdish language. The holiday is observed on March 21 or 22, the time of the spring equinox. Nowruz celebrates the rebirth of nature and the victory of light over the darkness of the long, cold winter.

Left: Kurdish women near Mosul, Iraq, wear colorful clothes for Nowruz.

Left: Iraqi Kurds living near Baghdad celebrate Nowruz.

Nowruz Bonfire

The Nowruz bonfire is one of the most exciting Nowruz traditions. Kurdish families gather large piles of wood on the day before Nowruz. In the evening, they make a bonfire. They gather around the fire and give thanks for having survived the barren winter months. As the night draws on, people jump over the flames of the bonfire. They sing songs, asking for good health in the coming year. Other Nowruz traditions include the Seven Wishes and the Thirteenth Day, which are of Persian origin and celebrated by Iranian Kurds.

The Seven Wishes of Nowruz

A few weeks before Nowruz, Iranian Kurds set up a special table. It holds seven different items, each symbolizing a New Year's wish. The seven items all begin with the letter *s*. They are vinegar *(serekh)*, a Persian candy called *samanu*, a gold coin called a *sekeh*, a hyacinth flower *(sonbol)*, fruits *(senjed)*, green vegetables *(sabzee)*, and garlic *(seer)*. These items stand for kindness and generosity, peace and justice, positive and clear thoughts, truth, good works toward others, prosperity, and eternal life.

Above: Kurdish musicians perform Nowruz music at a folk festival in Wales, England.

THE THIRTEENTH DAY

On the thirteenth day after Nowruz, Iranian Kurdish families go on a picnic, complete with games and fun celebrations. This holiday is called Sizdah Bedar. The Kurds consider thirteen an unlucky number. By celebrating on the thirteenth day of the year, they hope keep to unlucky things from happening.

GLOSSARY

archaeologists: scientists who study the remains of past human cultures

assimilate: to blend in with the traditions and lifestyle of the dominant population

cuneiform: a type of writing that consists of wedge-shaped characters carved into clay or stone tablets; used by the ancient Babylonians, Akkadians, Persians, and other similar groups

daf (DAHF): a handheld drum

deforestation: the clearing or death of trees in a forest

dialect: a regional variation on a main language

emir: a Kurdish chief; also used to refer to a prince, commander, or head of state in some Islamic countries

equinox: a day of the year when there are the equal hours of daytime and nighttime; usually occurring about March 21 and September 21

gourani (goo-RAH-nee): Kurdish songs that are based on poems and sung on both everyday and special occasions

grammar: the rules and structure of a language

guerilla war: irregular warfare waged by small groups of soldiers

hydroelectricity: electric power generated by the force of rushing water

migratory: traveling from the place to place in search of food or breeding grounds

mosaic: a picture or decoration made of small, usually colored pieces of inlaid stone or glass

nomads: people who travel from place to place, without a permanent home

Nowruz (now-ROSE): the Kurdish New Year

seismic zone: an area that is prone to have earthquakes

tanbur (tahn-BOOR): a pear-shaped instrument that is plucked or strummed

FINDING OUT MORE

Books

Bodnarchuk, Ann. *Kurdistan: Region Under Siege.* Minneapolis, MN: Lerner Publications Company, 2000.

Bruni, Mary Ann Smothers, Ali Alatas, and Texas Memorial Museum. *Journey through Kurdistan.* Austin, TX: University of Texas Press, 1997.

King, John. *Kurds.* New York, NY: Thomson Learning, 1994.

Laird, Elizabeth. *Kiss the Dust.* New York, NY: Dutton Children's Books, 1992.

Meiselas, Susan, and Martin van Bruinessen. *Kurdistan: In the Shadow of History.* New York, NY: Random House, 1997.

Sabbah, Ann Carey. *Kurds.* Mankato, MN: Smart Apple Media, 1999.

Videos

Ancient Mesopotamia. Schlessinger Media, 1998.

Good Kurds, Bad Kurds. Kevin McKiernan, 2000.

Websites

<http://www.akakurdistan.com>

<http://www.knn.u-net.com>

<http://www.krg.org>

<http://www.kurdishlibrary.org>

<http://www.kurdistanpress.com>

<http://www.kurdmedia.com>

<http://www.middleeastuk.com/com/kcc>

Organizations

American Kurdish Information Network (AKIN)
2600 Connecticut Avenue NW, #1
Washington, DC 20008-1558
Tel: (202) 483-6444
E-mail: akin@kurdistan.org
Website: <http://www.kurdistan.org>

Kurdish Human Rights Project
Suite 319, Linen Hall
162–168 Regent Street
London W1R 5TB
United Kingdom
Tel: (44) 207-287-2772
E-mail: khrp@khrp.demon.co.uk
Website: <http://www.khrp.org>

INDEX

ABOUT THE AUTHORS

Anthony C. LoBaido is a staff writer for WorldNetDaily.com. He has visited Kurdistan and written many articles on the Kurds of Iraq, Turkey, and Europe. He is based in New York. Yumi Ng is a writer/editor who has a strong interest in indigenous peoples. She has worked on book projects ranging from the Yanomami of South America to the Zulu of Africa. Paul A. Rozario is a student of religion, specializing in Ethiopian Christianity, and has worked with indigenous peoples in the field. The publishers would like to thank BBC journalist Hiwa Osman and the Kamkars Group for their help with this book.

PICTURE CREDITS

(B=bottom; C=center; F= far; I=inset; L=left; M=main; R=right; T=top)

AFP: 17TL, 35B, 41T, 45T • Atlas/Geographic: 7T, 26T, 27T, 28M, 29BR, 30M, 32TL, 35TL, 37TR, 39CR, 39BL, 42TL • Bes Stock: 3BR, 10M • Camera Press: 19CR, 31T • Getty Images/Hulton Archive: 29TL, 36-37M, 43T • Hiwa Osman: 25BR, 40M, 41BL • Hutchison Picture Library: 2T, 8M, 21TL, 21BR, 23BR, 24M, 24 TL, 31BL, 32-33M, 33CL • Jiham Ammar / The Kamkars Group: 36TL • John R. Jones: 11BR • Nazima Kowall: 26M, 34M, 42M • Nik Wheeler: 27BR, 44M • Sonia Halliday Photographs: 6-7M, 7CR, 12M, 13BR, 15TL • Topham Picturepoint: 4M, 13TL, 14M, 15CR, 20-21M, 22-23M, 33TR • Travel Ink: cover, 46BR • Trip Photographic Library: title page, 9TL, 9BR, 11T, 16M, 18M, 25T, 38M, 39TL, 45BR